The Journey to Self-Love

Melissa Fredericks

This has truly been a dream come true! It wouldn't have been possible without the help of some pretty important people in my life!

1) God! Thank you for allowing me to find purpose in my tears! For years, I felt forgotten about and like I didn't have a purpose in this life. But, this book is the manifestation that you're intentional and my purpose was by design! Thank you for reminding me of your everlasting love toward me!

2) My husband, my Kevy! If you know anything about Kevin, then you know he wants to be the best at everything he does, and that includes being a husband. He has been my sounding board, encourager, motivator, and inspiration through this entire process! I love you so very much and I thank you for pushing me outside of my comfort zone.

3) My friends! There were only a few people I trusted to read my book prior to its release, and to those people: thank you for being in my inner circle! I trust you and your judgement, so if the book sucks, it's your fault!

4) My family! Your unconditional love and encouragement was everything to me!

5) My editor! This goes without saying! Thank you for riding with me!!

6) You, dear reader! Thank you for following me on this journey and trusting me enough to share a nugget of wisdom that might encourage you to change your life!

Table of Contents

Melissa Fredericks

Introduction:

Love yourself. Two very simple words, but when coupled together, they are actually quite complex. Here is the definition that I created for Self-Love: The ability to embrace every facet of your being with an unconditional love of who you are and an acceptance of who you are not. As I take you along this journey, you will find that genuine self-love produces a level of peace that comes from being content with the inward and outward perceptions of your self-image. I embarked on this journey some seven years ago to manifest self-love in my own life. I remember when the thought of loving myself felt like a "fixed battle" I was guaranteed to lose--an insurmountable task even. I thought there were far too many things wrong with me and there was no way I could fall in-love with myself. It seemed I would be plagued by low self-esteem my entire life and there was absolutely nothing I could do about it! But this is so far from the truth: There is absolutely something that can be done!

I write this book with two main purposes in mind: I hope you learn a little about me, but more importantly, my prayer is that you feel empowered, uplifted, and encouraged to come out of the rut that you may find yourself in right now. I hope you'll find the strength to take the necessary steps to change your life! The principles I discuss throughout the book are those that I have personally applied and they have indeed changed my life! My mother used to say: "There is a difference between 'head knowledge' and experience...And once you've experienced something, there is a certain conviction that comes along with knowing something that you've experienced first-hand..." As a fellow sojourner who has walked this path, crying tears along this road to self-love, I speak not only with conviction, but with authority, passion, and compassion. I've been on the "other-side," so I understand first-hand the undertaking you will have to endure to join me on this journey, and I know it will be the hardest thing you'll ever do, but make no mistake: The results will offer the greatest reward--the reward of falling in love with yourself. Learning to love yourself is the single most powerful thing you can do for yourself. Please don't be intimidated to take on the challenge; instead embrace it as a lifelong journey that will allow you the opportunity to reach your highest level of self.

I started this journey with a single mission: Raise my self-confidence and self-esteem. I was never driven by: vanity, conceitedness, or my ego. Falling in love with myself was about developing a genuine love and appreciation for me--All of me! It was about changing my perspective and choosing to focus on the good things that I have to offer instead of reducing myself to my flaws. After all, I was born and will eventually die in this skin, so why not love it?! Why not?! Why not look in the mirror and like who I see in the reflection? Not just my good heart and personality, but also my physical being: The person who others see. Why can't I like and love that person? Flaws and all.

Perhaps you're in a place in your life where you're not too fond of the person you see in the mirror; maybe you can visualize yourself accomplishing your heart's greatest desires, but you feel too inadequate to pursue them. In a word, you feel: stuck and you're not sure where or how to begin. It's easy for life to "become a blur" with our daily routines and to lose ourselves in the various roles of womanhood (i.e.: wife, girlfriend, mom, daughter, sister, leader, employee, entrepreneur) that we play. Each of these roles should be held in high-esteem, but there is something to be said about feeling like a woman--a confident woman who can go out and "take on life by the horns" and then turn around and look in the mirror and feel like God's Masterpiece--fearfully and wonderfully made (Psalm 139:14, New International Version). I know at one time, I desired to feel this way, but it eluded me for many years. I had to make a conscious decision to make a change--a change that would grant me the courage, strength, and confidence to walk into my destiny unafraid and unashamed of who I am.

By the end of this book, my ultimate goal is to help someone to be bold and inspired enough to initiate your own "campaigns" (personal missions of self-discovery and confidence building; more on that as your journey through this book continues) to do all that you can to evolve into the best version of yourself! If I can do it, believe me: You can too! My passion and past experiences of low self-esteem combined have "fueled" my desire to help other women transform into all that they desire to be. I pray that you experience the complete and supernatural healing and renewal of your: mind, body, and soul--perfect gifts from the years of negative self-talk you've been self-inflicting by speaking over yourself.

The Journey to Self Love

Confirmation

My husband (Kevin) and I have a podcast called: *The Love Hour*. In a more personal episode of the podcast, entitled: "For Women Only" (Episode 11 of *The Love Hour*), I shared my personal struggle with low self-esteem and overcoming insecurities in the bedroom. I was as honest and transparent as I've ever been...And terrified! I was putting myself in a very vulnerable position by opening my heart to people I'd never met. While it has always been a passion of mine to encourage women, I must admit that Kevin is my "security blanket." He's the big personality most people know: A natural in front of people and the camera, and while I don't get "stage fright," I am very "camera shy." I wasn't only sharing my story for the world to hear, I was doing it alone...But it's so funny how God works! I was able to overcome some of my fears, while simultaneously helping women and being affirmed in what I know God has called me to do.

The love and support I received from the "For Women Only" episode was overwhelming, I must admit. I was encouraged even more by the number of women who could relate to what I went through. Then, to "top it all off," my "campaigns" became a movement in and of themselves! (For clarity's sake: My "campaigns" are a focused period of time that I dedicate to "loving-on" a particular area of myself. In each "campaign," I "tackle" a different dynamic of personal insecurity and I work diligently in that area to become a better me). A number of the episode's female listeners decided to apply some of the principles of my story to their own lives, which was absolutely encouraging! (To this day, I receive amazing testimonies from women via email and social media regarding the episode's impact).

It has always been my heart's desire to encourage and up-lift women and the podcast's "For Women Only" episode especially allowed me the opportunity to do just that! And moreover, it confirmed the calling on my life-- the calling to encourage and uplift women. Honestly: It was "high time" I answer the call. As a result, I began to seriously consider writing a book. After years of sitting in the background (which is totally fine by me), I decided it was time for me to step into all that God has created me to do. This book is the first step...

So let the journey begin!

Am I Pretty?

My mom and dad married when I was a baby, so I grew up in a two-parent home. I'm the oldest of three girls and my father treated us like queens. There was nothing my parents wouldn't do for us.

When I was about eight years old, my mom gave her life to Jesus Christ and became very active in the church. She was "on fire" for God and became very strict with me and my sisters. We couldn't spend the night at our friends' houses, we didn't attend school dances, we didn't listen to secular music, and the list goes on from there. Eventually, my dad got saved as well, but my mom was always the spiritual leader in our home.

Even at a young age, I took my salvation very seriously. I wasn't known to be a person who cursed. My mom used to tell me and my sisters that cursing was very "un-ladylike" and I wanted to be a lady, so I didn't curse. I wasn't allowed to date until I was 16, and outside of the one guy I dated, I kept true to that rule. I was pretty much a good girl! I remember watching a movie on TV and the actress said she wanted the first guy she kissed to be her husband, and for some reason, I thought that was a great idea: I wanted that to be my reality too! Yeah: I was a "good girl."

I realize now that growing up the way I did has had both a positive and negative impact on me as an adult. For instance, I have standards and morals that I hold myself to that many others may not; however, growing up with the entrenched "good girl" mentality also had a negative impact on me that I wouldn't realize until much later on.

You see, when you grow up as a "good girl," you can convince yourself that "holiness" equates to being: small, asexual, and looking very homely (or even matronly), all in an effort to represent Christ and not attract the wrong kind of attention...And, for a long time, I subconsciously subscribed to this notion. I would "shrink myself and my gifts" in public in an attempt to be humble. I wouldn't allow myself to accept that I could be or accomplish anything great. I impeded my own greatness. The *Bible* says that we are created in the image of God (Genesis 1:27, New International Version) and I serve an incredibly great God, therefore I have greatness in me! This was the truth I needed to stand on, but I didn't and as a result, I began to develop feelings of: fear, insecurity, and inadequacy. I often felt inferior. While I knew I had a God-given ability to teach, I wasn't secure enough in the skin He had given me to fully step out into destiny. I didn't feel like the "masterpiece" that God created with a purpose in this life. Feelings of low self-esteem began to emerge. I felt insignificant and small and to be frank: I felt ugly. Not the "cute ugly" where you feel cute most days, with a few bad days, but the ugly where you look in the mirror and you dislike the reflection staring back at you.

I recall crying on some days, wondering why God made me this way: small framed-body, acne-prone face, hair that disgusted me, a wide nose, standard brown eyes, big lips, crooked teeth, and this chocolate skin! You name it--I didn't like it and I wanted to change it. I often found myself questioning: Am I pretty? When other people see me, what do they see? What do they say about me behind my back? Am I good enough? Am I...Am I ugly? These thoughts were terrifying and they plagued me for much of my life. I wore low self-esteem like a garment. You could see "it" all over me: in my demeanor, my clothing, the way I treated myself, and the way I interacted with other people. Low self-esteem managed to penetrate every area of my life. I was afraid to try new things, I was constantly concerned with what other people thought about me, and it even affected my marriage. I found myself paralyzed by my own destructive thinking. For years, I was unhappy with my physical appearance and the state of my life, which carried over from childhood into my teenage years--even into adulthood. It wasn't until much later in life that I was able to identify where those feelings stemmed from; when I did, I created an action plan to combat years of negative self-imagery and self-rejection that I had inflicted upon myself.

The Journey to Self Love

Melissa Fredericks

The Message and The Messenger

During my college years, I went home every Friday to spend the weekend with my family and attend church on Sunday. I remember one particular Friday, I was picked up by my friend's mom. My friend and I stayed in the same dorm, so when her mom arrived, we walked downstairs and jumped in the car. Immediately upon entering the car, the mother told her daughter, "You look pretty" and then she turned to me and said, "Melissa you look ugly." My friend's mom immediately followed it up with "I'm just kidding," but the damage was already done. By this time, I was in my late teens/early 20s, and looking back on it, I already suffered from low self-esteem, so her comment only helped to "cement" those feelings of low self-worth. (...And, yes, this experience is definitely something that still affects me to this very day). The mother of my friend may have been joking, (although to a certain degree, I believe she was being serious), but the words she spoke only reinforced the negative view I had on myself. I cannot hold her fully accountable for my esteem issues, but her words did hurt me badly.

After much self-reflection on the various aspects of my life, I've come to the conclusion that: I was a casualty of society's definition of beauty long before this incident in college. I had pretty much gone through my entire life feeling defeated in self-esteem and the odd thing is, I could never pinpoint where it started. You would think that growing up the way that I did--in a two-parent home with my biological father who was very reassuring of my beauty as a child--I wouldn't have been susceptible to feelings of low self-esteem, but I was and in fact struggled with it for a number of years. So what was it? Where did these feelings begin? I believe I accepted the idea that I didn't fit into the mainstream definition of beauty. I'm certainly not the pretty "light-skinned" black girl with light brown eyes and long, flowing hair. Me? No! I'm just a regular ol' black girl with absolutely nothing special about me (so I thought). I now look at myself differently, but it took years before I began to truly appreciate the uniqueness that God gave to me.

Speaking of mainstream beauty: One Saturday afternoon, I decided to watch a documentary called, *Miss Representation*[1]. The documentary essentially highlights sexism in the media and in Hollywood. During the documentary, several women (who hold different positions in the media and Hollywood) are interviewed and offer their insight into the disparaging treatment of men versus women. Pat Mitchell's (President & CEO of Paley Center for Media and Former President, CEO of PBS) interview "struck" as she remarked that: "The media is the message and the messenger and an increasingly powerful one…"

Upon hearing this, I realized the "gravity" of her words as I took a moment to think about some of the factors that can influence a child's self-esteem: Negative self-talk, unhealthy (even traumatizing) childhood experiences, and of course, the media. With the advent of all-things social media, the impact is so much more significant than in years past. For instance, today's teens and young adults spend a considerable amount of time consuming images via social media networks, invariably comparing their lives with what they see; the unfortunate result is when those of the next generation feel as if their lives don't measure up with the lives of others, feelings of low self-esteem are "on ripe ground to sprout." Then it occurred to me: While my childhood was during the 90s and social media was not a "thing" during that time, various forms of media (serving as both "the message and the messenger") still had a significant impact on me as a young, impressionable little girl. What little girl doesn't want to feel pretty? Part of a child's identity development involves being frequently affirmed in a positive light by those he or she looks up to (and in many cases: she's raised by). Sadly, I don't recall too many brown-skinned women being defined as and celebrated for their beauty. The narrow view of beauty that sidelined dark-skinned women, heavily influenced the way in which I saw myself. Based on parameters set by society (that I believed to be an absolute truth), I was the opposite of the definition of beauty and acutely aware of this fact. This became the foundation that gave life to my feelings of low self-esteem.

I recognize that while I share my story, your childhood may have been completely different, but perhaps you have an experience from your childhood that shaped and changed the trajectory of your life because of its impact. Before we go any further: Take a moment to forgive anyone and all who left you wounded. Even if their intention was malicious, holding onto a grudge only hinders your progress and ability to move on with your life. Maybe as you're reading this, you're taking inventory of your life and you can't pinpoint an event (that) or individual (who) may have affected your self-esteem, or maybe the culprit is you, or maybe it's society. Still, I encourage you to forgive. Forgive yourself for not believing you would ever measure up or for comparing yourself to others and being terribly convinced that you're not good enough. Forgiveness will allow you to go into this journey unburdened with thoughts of anyone else, especially because you'll need to be as "light" as possible for this journey ahead. You'll need to be consumed with thoughts of positivity in order for a transformation to occur. Embark on your self-love journey with a clean heart and pure intentions because doing so will only amount to a better you in the end, and isn't that the ultimate goal? To become a better you?

Point-of-Reflection: Are you harboring feelings of unforgiveness from experiences from your childhood? Sometimes in life you have to accept an apology you've never been given. Take this moment to forgive those who may have hurt you in the past.

Encouragement: We all have insecurities that we deal with. Know that you're not alone in this journey of loving yourself!

A New & Improved Me!

Let's take a "trip down memory lane" for a moment: Do you remember the show on TLC called *What Not to Wear*₁? I used to love this show! There were two hosts (Clinton and Stacy) and they would take an unsuspecting "victim" on a shopping spree and revamp his/her wardrobe. While Clinton and Stacy went shopping with their "victims," they explained how to select versatile clothing items for each week's comings and goings. I didn't realize it then, but this show became the catalyst and a metaphor for my journey of self-love.

By the end of each episode of *What Not to Wear*, the "victims" experienced more than just a shopping spree: A transformation took place on the inside. Each transformation included a professional hair and makeup experience as part of the "big reveal," where the participant would surprise their family and loved ones with their new look. By the end, the show's participants always had greater self-esteem than when the show started: They had more strut in their walk, looked happier, and were far more confident! This change, this inward feeling of confidence that exudes outwardly is what I wanted!

...So I embarked on a series of "campaigns" (as I call them)--intentional personal missions to build my self-confidence from the inside out. I began with how I felt about myself on the inside: I started with inner monologues and changed my self-talk and eventually, I began to change on the outside. Starting inwardly was a pivotal part of my transformation because in order to feel different about myself, it was important to change my perspective about me and then I could look in the mirror and like who I saw as a result of a mature perspective.

John P. Hewitt notes the following in the *Oxford Handbook of Positive Psychology*2: "In sociology and psychology, self-esteem reflects a person's overall subjective emotional evaluation of his or her own worth. It is a judgment of one's self, as well as an attitude toward the self."

Self-esteem is an *emotional* evaluation of one's own worth. Did you "catch that?" An *emotional* evaluation. It's emotional because it's based on your perception of yourself, therefore you have the power to change and even create a new perception of yourself. In short: you hold the power to directly influence your self-esteem! That's right! You have the power! Once you change and mature your perspective of yourself--meaning every "fiber" of your being--you'll end up positively impacting your self-esteem. I'll tell you why this is so powerful: A lot of times, we victimize ourselves, giving in to the lies of the Enemy himself (otherwise known as Satan), who hopes that we (as women especially) never live out our unique purpose in the Earth. To be clear: I'm not discounting a painful experience from your past. I recognize that trauma can permanently alter who you are and who you could potentially become. I know this to be true because I've had experiences that have forever changed me, so I get it! But what I want you to understand is that you don't have to take ownership of the victim mentality or title! You're not powerless! In fact, you can take back the power from your accuser and take your life back into your own hands! The choice is yours: You can take ownership of your life and allow no one to hold power over you or you can continue to wallow in the "comfort zone" of self-pity. The choice is yours!f You can change the course of your life for the better! I encourage you, as of this very moment, to dictate and control your happiness. Give yourself the opportunity to be elevated to reach your full potential.

The Journey to Self Love

Campaign: "You are Worth It"

When I turned 27 (a few years ago), I don't know what went off in my brain, but I had finally decided "NO MORE!" I no longer wanted to go out in public feeling embarrassed when I saw someone unexpectedly because I wasn't dressed "up to par." (You know we've all had that encounter). I no longer wanted to attend events with my husband and feel like he wasn't proud to have me on his arm. I decided I wanted a change!

...So I started buying clothes and doing different things for myself. I was trying to *buy* my confidence with material things, but that approach didn't last long. I couldn't figure out what I was doing wrong! I was attempting to to re-create my own *What Not to Wear* episode, but I went about it totally wrong. You see: I didn't realize that I had years of negative declarations to "purge" from "every fiber of my being." Sadly enough, I started to believe and accept that I wasn't enough. I wasn't pretty. I wasn't adequate. And the worst part is that I believed I never would be.

I decided I had to first make a change with my self-talk exchanges. Self-talk (or "inner monologues" as I like to call them) consists of the conversations you have with yourself--either aloud or mentally--about yourself. Regardless of if your "inner monologues" are spoken aloud or mentally-derived, the words and/or thoughts have the power to become your reality. So, here are my questions for you: How do you talk to yourself? What is your tone like? Are you kind to yourself? Are you your biggest fan or are you your biggest critic? Think about all of this for a moment. If I'm being honest, there was time when my "inner monologues" were entirely negative. I would stand on my metaphorical "soap box" and "tear myself down" by criticizing and critiquing my: physical, mental, and emotional traits. No wonder I felt so badly about myself! In my "class of one," I taught myself that I wasn't a deserving candidate of the best of anything.

I'm sure you've heard the childhood nursery rhyme: "Sticks and stones may break my bones, but words will never hurt me." However, the alarming fact is: Words can and often do hurt and their scars can be felt years after the words are spoken. As I mentioned, at this time, my "inner monologues" were almost exclusively negative. They often consisted of me reinforcing the idea that I would never fit into society's definition of beauty. "You're not good enough." "You'll never be perceived as pretty by others." "There is nothing special about you!" "This is all life has to offer." "Happiness will forever elude you." This daily dose of negativity poisoned my mind, so when I tried to make a change, I couldn't because I was stuck in my toxic state of mind. I had to re-condition my entire mentality. I began with where it all started: My internal perception and evaluation of myself. The thoughts and conversations I was having with myself had to change.

I've pointed out the role the media played in the development of my self-esteem (or lack thereof), but in full transparency: The media may have planted the seed, but I certainly tended to and watered the seed over the years. I became my biggest critic. I mastered pointing out my flaws and shortcomings. I had become an expert in negative self-talk, and in turn, I began to manifest feelings of low self-worth and low self-esteem.

As a child, my mom used to admonish my sisters and I to "speak life," relative to Proverbs 18:21, which speaks about the power of death and life being in our tongue. And it's so true! Your thoughts become your words, your words become your actions, and your actions become your life's patterns. The more disciplined you become in being aware of your negative and unpleasant "inner monologues," the sooner and more consistently a better reality will manifest in your various life seasons.

According to experts, there is a "magic ratio" of 5:1 necessary for an absolute mindset shift. In theory, this "magic ratio" means we need five positive thoughts to eliminate a single negative thought.

...So I developed a very simple reminder: I am worth it. I had to "starve the negativity" that I'd declared over myself for years and start cultivating a more positive mindset: The mindset that simply said, "I am worth it." Not only did I have to say it, I had to start believing it. I had to believe what God says about me (in His Word). I stopped buying clothes and literally went on a journey of changing my mind about myself on the inside. I would wake up in the morning and literally tell myself aloud: "I am worth it. As is. Without change and without exception!" This was my mantra for months. I didn't need material possessions: clothes, shoes, or makeup to validate worth it. I had to wholeheartedly believe that I was. I had to look in the mirror and believe the words: I. Am. Worth. It. Even when I didn't feel my best--I am worth it. As is. Without change and without exception. Not only worth it, but *worthy*: Worthy to receive love from others and most importantly, worthy to receive love from myself! I re-trained my mind to believe that I was also worthy of treating myself to nice things and even worthy of feeling good about myself: Feeling confident in my skin! And guess what? So are you! The truth is that placing limitations on the love I showed to myself only further diminished my self-worth and lowered my self-esteem, and this was counterproductive to what I was trying to achieve. I made it my mission to change my negative inner dialogues and replace it with: I am worth it. As is. Without change. Without exception.

I must admit, this was not easy. The hardest part about repeating those words to myself in the beginning was that I didn't feel like they were true. I didn't wholeheartedly believe. In fact, I felt like I was lying to myself. The truth was that I didn't feel worthy and there were plenty of things I wanted to change. I memorized all the things I wanted to change about myself and could recite them in an "elevator speech"--30 seconds flat--but I had to stay the course, despite my feelings. Your beliefs influence your feelings and your feelings dictate your behavior. Changing my belief system was of paramount importance to directly affecting my self-esteem. I had to intentionally and systematically recondition my mind to believe in my own value and worth. And sure enough, I began to "feel" differently. Nothing changed on the outside, but there was definitely a distinct detectable change occurring on the inside.

During the transformation, I wasn't able to articulate what was happening, but I eventually read the book, *The Power of Charm*[1], by Brian Tracy and Ron Arden, and the authors detail exactly what I experienced. The *Power of Charm* is about learning to be a captivating and charming speaker, but included is a chapter dedicated to encouraging the readers to visualize and then mechanically act in a "charming" way, until the principles discussed in the book become a seamless and a natural part of your being. Tracy and Arden call this the "act as if" principle. The principle basically states that if you "act as if" you already feel a particular way, your actions will soon trigger the feelings to go with them.

In modern day colloquialism, this would be termed: "Fake it until you make it!" Well, that's essentially the "act as if" principle and that's essentially what I did. I had to "act as if" I was worth it, even when I didn't particularly feel like I was. On days that I felt awful--actually, especially on days that I felt awful--I had to tell myself that I was worth it and treat myself as such. Your mind and body will respond to whatever you accept as truth, so until you can believe it, treat yourself "as if" you are worth it and eventually, your inner confessions will be made manifest in every facet of your outward demeanor.

It's important to note that your personal declarations (statements of affirmation) become self-fulfilling prophecies. The way you treat yourself will influence the way you feel and vice versa. So when you tell yourself that you're beautiful, worthy, and valuable, your subconscious believes those affirmations and in turn, this will affect your demeanor and you will begin to treat yourself as such. And the inverse is true. When you tell yourself you're inadequate and worthless, you'll feel inadequate and the corresponding behavior will follow. But, this isn't all bad news! All this means this that the power lies solely in your hands!

You can build your self-esteem simply by adopting actions and philosophies that will increase and build your self-esteem. It really is that simple and unfortunately that difficult. There will be days when you don't feel like getting dressed or made up, etc., but even on those days you have to remember that you're worth it. As is and without exception. The only way to change your mind about yourself is through the repeated actions of "acting as if" you are worth it. Those repeated actions of cultivating your self-worth will literally become the "building blocks" to re-building your self-esteem.

Point-of-Reflection: What do your inner dialogues consist of? Are they negative or positive? Decide to be vigilant in changing the tone of the conversations you have with yourself, about yourself.

Encouragement: I need you to remember: "You are worth it--As is...Without change...Without exception."

The "Love On" Challenge

At the end of the "You Are Worth It" "campaign," which was about affirming myself, it was time to act! Obviously, just thinking and visualizing that I was enough, wasn't enough. Doing it--acting on my new belief system--was the key to enforcing it. One of the easiest ways to measure how much you love yourself is to evaluate how you treat yourself. The way in which you treat yourself is a direct reflection of your self-esteem. It was time I started treating myself in a loving manner!

As women, we often put ourselves last on "the totem pole." We take good care of so many people, but making ourselves a priority is never a priority. We often feel guilty if we go out shopping and indulge in a little personal "retail therapy." We feel guilty if we buy something expensive (of great value and quality), even if we have the money to do so. As women, especially mothers, we buy into this idea that a great mother must look exhausted and unkempt--as if there is no way a woman can take care of herself and also take care of her household. But I'm here to tell you: You can do both and the repercussion of not taking care of yourself is something you simply can't afford to risk. Do away with feelings of guilt and the belief that self-deprivation and self-sacrifice are the definitions of woman and motherhood and replace them with the actuality that making yourself a priority benefits not only you, but your family as well.

I deliberately put aside those feelings of guilt and behaved in such a way that enforced my "I am worth it" mantra. I would go shopping and tell myself, "Melissa you're worth buying something for yourself today. You're worth buying these shoes you've been 'eyeballing' for weeks, hoping they'd go on sale, but haven't." (To be clear, I wasn't being irresponsible with my money and I'm not suggesting that you be either, but a lot of times, we have the finances or resources to treat ourselves, but don't due to a sense of guilt). I had to change my perspective that convinced me that neglecting my own needs somehow made me a better wife and mother. What a lie?! The moment a woman feels better about herself, she automatically becomes a better woman to those around her. The individuals closest to you reap the benefits of you feeling good about yourself because your confidence and increased self-esteem permeate every area of your life just as the opposite is true. Conversely, a negative self-image can make you feel "trapped" in a life and body you wish you could change. You'll be bound from trying new things, even something as simple as taking a picture! (Yes, I've been there too! I used to hate taking pictures because I never wanted to reminisce on moments captured-in-time that simply reminded me of my feelings of low self-worth).

I truly had to believe and then act on the belief that I was worth getting up a little earlier in the morning so I would have time to put in the effort to look my best before leaving the house. Sometimes I felt sleeping in was worth more than the confidence that would be instilled in me from a new and improved morning routine. But on days when I decided to sleep in, I felt awful, and without fail: I would run into someone looking a "hot mess" and the cycle of negative self-talk would try to creep in and overtake the positive affirmations I had begun. I certainly didn't want to start at "ground zero" again, because I could see and feel the progress I was making.

Changing your behavior is the real test because it requires a lot more discipline, dedication, and in so many ways, becomes the "litmus test" for your conviction in your new confessions. Do your beliefs take you only as far as you have to act on them or can you carry out what you believe? I was determined to carry it out!

As I entered into the outward part of my transformation, I actually a started a "Love On" campaign to go along with this phase of action. The "Love On" campaign" was where I picked a physical feature about myself and decided to "highlight" that feature for a week. You'd be surprised how much confidence begins to develop when you focus on the things you like about yourself versus those you don't (but can eventually learn to love anyway). I must admit, it was hard because there weren't too many things I liked about myself, but I was determined to choose one thing and hone in on that one thing. I chose my eyes: They were the one thing that I've always loved. I wanted to accentuate my eyes to the best of my ability and what better way than with makeup? But my makeup skills needed work.

I remember watching *Keeping Up with the Kardashians*[1] (one of their earlier seasons) and Kim sharing a story about when she and her sisters started wearing makeup. The story goes that their father enrolled them in a makeup school (of sorts) so they could learn the proper techniques for applying makeup. For whatever reason, this story resonated with me. I didn't want to just apply eyeshadow; my overall goal was to "love on" my eyes and highlight them as my best feature, so I needed them to look their best! So I started watching makeup tutorials and teaching myself how to properly apply eyeshadow. I wanted to focus on my eyes as much as possible since they were the one feature I absolutely adored about myself. I decided to go to a MAC counter to buy: eyeshadow, eyeliner, and brushes. I'll never forget: I walked out with: Woodwinked and Twinks eyeshadows, an eyeshadow brush, a blending brush, and an eyeliner brush. Little did I know that this would be the beginning of an endless "love affair" that I still currently have with makeup.

Some of you may be thinking that makeup is self-absorbed and that its application only focuses on a woman's exterior and her physical appearance and the resulting confidence is superficial. However, I assure you: It's much deeper than that! Can you recall the last time you had your makeup professionally done? Or the last time you applied false lashes or even lipstick? Think about the confidence you felt that day. To me, that's what it's about: Walking out of the house and feeling "fly!" It's about feeling: good, comfortable, and confident in your skin. Many times we leave the house looking like "Who did it and why?" and what we don't realize is that our overall demeanor is discernible to others. People can sense when you feel good just as much as they can sense when you feel down and low.

I was in pursuit of that "feel good" energy. I wanted to naturally (and effortlessly) exude confidence all the time! I wanted high self-esteem on a daily basis, but, life happens...I live in the "real world" and I understand that, oftentimes, life seems very mundane and we just don't have occasions to: get dressed up, put lashes on, and apply a full face of makeup--factors which all contribute to increasing your emotional evaluation of yourself (i.e.: self-esteem). So, I changed my definition of "occasion." As far as I'm concerned: I am enough of a reason. In fact, I am the reason AND the occasion!

We often think we have to wait for special occasions to look our best. How many "special events" do you attend on a regular basis? Probably not that many...So why do you have to wait to look and feel your best? Create occasions to look your best--for yourself! I often take a little special time on Friday's to do my makeup. I literally go to work and then home fully made up! It may seem unnecessary to some, but it reinforces the notion that I am worth it. These small behavior patterns reinforce my positive affirmations, and when you add them all up, they result in a life change: A change that allows me to live a much more fulfilled and happier life!

Perhaps this isn't practical for you to get fully made up because of your profession, but don't let that be your excuse! Weekends will always exist and are the perfect excuse to create for getting dressed up! If you're married, I highly encourage you to celebrate your upcoming anniversary (a tip for another book, but for now, know that you should definitely be celebrating your anniversary), by getting all made up! Single Ladies: Get together with your girlfriends and plan: a fun, grown-up slumber party weekend, "staycation" in your city, or whatever esteem-boosting activities and events you find yourselves putting together that leave you feeling beautifully amazing--inside and out! Just know that you don't have to "break the bank!" All you've got to do is CREATE (and enjoy) the occasion!

Can I challenge you to partake in the "Love On" Challenge? I dare you! Take a week and actually show love to whatever your favorite feature is about yourself. For example, if you love your eyes, invest in your preferred makeup products and "play up" your eyes during the week of your choice. If you love your eyelashes, apply mascara to them this week to make them extra-long and thick! Perhaps you love your lips: Buy some lipstick and own it (I love a purple lipstick on brown girls! You can never go wrong!) Perhaps it's your cheeks! I have super high cheek bones and I used to HATE them! (Do you know contouring exists because women would "kill" to have naturally high cheekbones?) The point is to LOVE WHAT YOU HAVE! Clearly this isn't an exhaustive list: You could love your: Nails, Feet, Dimples... And the list could go on. Again: The point is to LOVE ON SOMETHING! The impact on your self-esteem that week will "sky rocket!" When you feel amazing, this very energy will naturally radiate from you.

Points-of-Reflection:
1) What is/are your favorite feature(s)? "Love on" that/ those feature(s) for a week (Much longer is even better)! Remember that feeling! It's something you'll want to replicate over and over. And when you do: Bask in the feeling of high self-esteem.

2) Now: Look through your closet and that dress you've had forever but you've never had an event to wear it to...Yeah, that one! Create the occasion for an upcoming weekend! Text your husband and let him know you're planning a date night where you'll both get dressed and go out...Just because! And if you're not married, text your girls and tell them that you're going on a "Girls' Night Out" and everyone is to get dressed up and look their best! Not only is life about creating occasions to enjoy each breath we are graced with, but life is about the memories we create from its everyday and extraordinary moments!

Encouragement: We all have things we don't like about ourselves, but remember: You can choose to focus on the negative or you can focus on the positive. Take this week and focus on the positive. And, if you want to get dressed-up for no particular occasion, remember: You are enough of a reason.

Melissa Fredericks

The Journey to Self Love

Melissa Fredericks

Campaign: "Get Sexy!"

Oh, the "Get Sexy" campaign: One of my favorite "campaigns!" This is where the fun begins! (And if you're wondering, yes, I actually named these campaigns as I was going through the journey because doing so helped me to identify exactly what I was focusing on and to fully concentrate on that specific area). I called this campaign, "Get Sexy," because I was overhauling my wardrobe and getting rid of all the clothes that made me feel "blah."

Case-in-Point: Eva Mendes did an interview a few years ago and she was quoted as saying, "...sweatpants, no no no...you can't do sweatpants... Ladies, number one cause of divorce in America, sweatpants—No, you can't do that!" Now of course, she is clearly exaggerating because the number one cause of divorce is not sweatpants, BUT ladies: Our men are visually stimulated... And I don't know about you, but I want to keep my man's eyes on ME--not only because I want to keep my husband's attention, but also because it is positive reinforcement for me! I'm not suggesting you go through a wardrobe overhaul for your husband because honestly, your reasoning needs to be better founded than that. Your husband should love you for you--regardless of any flaws you may have, and a good honorable husband will, but that doesn't mean he doesn't want to his woman to be happy in her own skin. One of the biggest realizations I had was the huge amount of satisfaction it brought to Kevin to see me so happy in my own skin. So, no: Wearing sweatpants will not send you straight to divorce court, but you'd be amazed at what NOT always wearing them can do for you and your marriage (or future marriage, for my single ladies out there who desire to be married).

So I set out to "get sexy!" Everything I ever wanted to try in terms of fashion, shoes, makeup, and even lingerie--I did it! I was determined to "break out of the "box" of limitations that I'd created for myself. For example, I used to believe that brown-skinned women couldn't wear blush. For some reason, I thought blush was only for white women. I also believed was that there were certain colors I could never wear because of my skin tone. For years, when I got a manicure, I would only get a French tip or cotton candy (you know: that light purple/pink/blue iridescent color?) because I felt I was too dark for anything else. Don't ask me where these thoughts originated from because I promise you: I have no clue. You wouldn't believe the number of blushes I own today: It really has become an obsession for me.

Again, these poorly founded "beauty reservations" just reinforced a negative self-image and low self-esteem. When you really break it down, you're telling yourself that you can't do something because of external qualities you obviously can't change. It makes you hate (or at the very least: want to change) that "thing" (i.e. my skin tone) about you. So when I went on this campaign, I was determined to get free from those thoughts!

In the season of my "Get Sexy" Campaign, I was asked to be on Erica Campbell's panel for her "More Than Pretty" conference she was hosting (if she ever hosts in your city, go!). I tried my best to get "fleeky" and decided to have my nails painted YELLOW. Yes girl: Yellow! I don't know if I'll ever do that again, but sometimes, I do crazy things like that to remind myself that I'm not limited by stupid fashion rules. Yes, there are certain colors that complement darker skin better than others, but you just have to find the right shades for you; you don't have to find yourself loyal to only one color.

What's so funny about this whole process is that I set out to develop high self-esteem and to feel better about myself, but I ended up with so much more! For example, during this "campaign," I learned the valuable lesson of being content in every facet of my life. I would find myself longing and wishing I had so and so's nose, or so and so's job, or their "fill in the blank." Can you relate? How many times have you mentally compared your life to someone else's and inevitably, you end up losing that battle? Whenever you do this, you only "rob yourself" of the opportunity to enjoy the journey that you're on! We never seem to measure up or have enough in comparison to someone else, so I made it a point to enjoy MY journey and MY process. In this conscious decision, I found so much contentment. We often search for happiness in people and inanimate objects, but true happiness is the result of an inward peace and contentment with YOUR life. Happiness can only occur when you stop comparing and start enjoying the life you've been given.

Now that I look back over my life, I realize there aren't many things I would change, even though I'd readily admit: I'm still a work-in-progress. I'm exactly where I am today because of those experiences! Given everything I've been through, I've found a passion for encouraging women to reach their full potential of greatness and helping them get through similar hurdles in life that I've already experienced! The only reason I am writing this book is because of those experiences.

The Journey to Self Love

Melissa Fredericks

The Social Media Era

We live in an age where if we don't post different facets of our daily lives on social media, then those things "didn't happen." Sometimes, it's hard not to be consumed with social media and feel the obligation to post everything! I'm guilty too! I still have to remind myself that it's okay to enjoy private moments without sharing them on a social media platform. Although social media relationships can have a positive effect on us, numerous studies have been conducted, linking social networking to depression and social isolation; eliciting feelings of envy, insecurity and poor self-esteem.

Social media is simply a "highlight reel" of life: "Highlight reel" being the operative phrase. Don't compare your bad days to someone's "highlight reel" of seemingly exciting moments. It's not fair to you. Social media can reinforce this notion of competition and comparison. I recall wishing my parents could afford to have a budget for my: nails, hair, and all of the latest name brand trends. I'm actually so grateful I'm not a teenager during this day and age. I couldn't imagine growing up trying to find my identity in a world where you're bombarded with images of what you should be. I had a hard enough time without social media! Even as an adult, I had to learn to get out of that "Keeping up with the Jones'" mentality. I know a lot of people who go "broke" trying to portray a certain image to others. Don't allow yourself to "fall into" this mentality and predicament.

Instagram is one of my favorite social media platforms. I love scrolling through pictures, and seeing a glimpse into the lives of people I've never met. [I'm no "ghost follower" either (a "ghost follower" is someone who just scrolls through Instagram, but never "likes" any of the pictures)]. I often "like" and compliment women on social media: We post pictures on a platform like Instagram for the likes after all! Many of us do it, just admit it! We all look for our "angles" and the best lighting to catch us just right to get the perfect selfie! (I still haven't perfected the art of taking a good selfie). ...But we have to ensure that our self-esteem isn't dependent on any outside factors. The value you place on yourself should not be "hinged upon" the opinions of others because people are fickle and will change at a moment's notice. The validation of others should not be the determining factor in how you feel about yourself.

Lessons Learned...

When I started on the journey of growing in self-confidence, I found myself buying clothes that were only name brand and feeling like I only wanted to wear items once for "The Gram"--Instagram that is. I had to stop and really evaluate the foundation of this transformation I was undertaking. I didn't want to look back on this period and realize I hadn't actually developed self-esteem at all, but that self-esteem that I thought I'd developed was actually based on material possessions. (Just in case I've not made myself clear: Material possessions are NOT what this journey is about. High self-esteem can't be bought with material things: It has to be a genuine and sincere re-evaluation of who you are). I recognized this and I wanted to feel good in my own skin because I felt good in my skin--not because of the name brand clothes or shoes I was wearing.

...So I even started a small "minimalist campaign" for myself. (Before you go "attacking" me about what it really means to be a minimalist, let me offer you my definition of-the-fact: I basically put a "freeze" on my spending habits. I wanted to ensure my self-esteem and -image weren't predicated on the designer of my clothes...Or that the only way I felt good about myself was if I was wearing something new). Clearly, I wasn't a traditional minimalist. I love a great bag, I readily admit to being a "makeup junkie," a great shoe "is LIFE," and a great outfit is pretty much what I live for! But on days where I decide not to do my makeup (because I have to clean my makeup brushes at some point, LOL!), or I'd rather just chill in sweatpants and a t-shirt, I wanted to make sure that even on those days: I felt good being Melissa--As I am, without change and without exception.

I hope this isn't a confusing message, but for the sake of clarity, let me try to put this very plainly: There is absolutely nothing wrong with getting dressed up and wearing the cutest outfit in your closet for the sake of just putting it on (and I encourage you to do that...this weekend! Don't wait!) Go ahead and put on a full face of makeup on Friday (or Monday or whenever!) just because you feel like it! There is also nothing wrong with treating yourself to an expensive (but within your budget; Remember: Fiscal responsibility is attractive!) outfit because that's what you want to do. The real question is: At the end of the day, when the makeup comes off and the outfit turns into pajamas and your hair is tied-up, can you look in the mirror and STILL love the person staring back at you? That's what it's about! It's about making sure our designer brand wardrobe (even a lavish lifestyle) isn't compensating for our low self-esteem. Let's not apply makeup to our faces because we're making up for our low self-image. Let's not buy expensive articles of clothing because we feel worthless without them. The moment you can appreciate all of you with AND without those things, then you know you've succeeded on this journey.

I wish I could tell you that you've reached the end. Your journey is now complete...After all, you have the tools to change your inner monologues and you know the steps to act on those changes, so that your outside matches how you feel on the inside. What else is left? Clearly, I can utter the magic word: Voila!...And all should be well. We should be cured right? But, not quite.

Yet another valuable lesson I learned during this phase was to simply say, "Thank You." Yes, those two simple words: Thank. You. I'll explain: When your self-esteem is low, it's easy to overlook the nice things people say about you. We don't believe it when someone says something nice. Instead, we think, "...yeah, but I'm not all that great..." and we "brush off" or even worse: Deflect the compliment. (Learn to give sincere compliments to others in return because it doesn't take away any of your shine when you do so). However, with that said, we must also learn to accept genuine compliments. I know at one time I was the "QUEEN" of deflecting a compliment. I would follow-up with something negative about myself. In fact, I STILL do that! I was once at an event and a lady complimented my hair and makeup and I HAD to bring up that my hair was a weave and I messed up filling in my eyebrow. WHY?! Why couldn't I have just said, "Thank you!" I'm still learning to truly appreciate compliments and take them to heart. Once again, I write this book not as an expert, but as someone who was "in your shoes" and sometimes, relapses back into her old habits.

Ultimately: You've got to learn to appreciate and not deflect compliments. Most of the time: People are being sincere... They're not being malicious or sarcastic, so if they compliment you, take it as such! You are worthy of these compliments! Yes, WORTHY! Which brings me to another lesson I learned.

The second lesson was about my intrinsic value. According to *Webster's Dictionary*[1], the definition of Intrinsic is: "Belonging to the essential nature or constitution of a thing," which basically means that you have value simply because you are. Consider a diamond ring: It is valuable simply because it's a diamond. You don't have to add any "bells or whistles" to it: It's valuable just by "being." Much like a diamond, you are valuable simply because you were created by God Himself--Creator of all Earthly beings and the universe itself. Isn't that powerful?! I get chills just thinking about it!

(As Americans especially...) Sometimes we place our value in all-things superficial and temporal: Materialistic possessions, socio-economic status, accomplishments, and the list goes on...But really, your value is simply in being you like no one else can and in the lives you impact for eternity.

Points-of-Reflection:
Let's pause for a moment and allow me to re-cap much of what's been said in the most recent chapters:

1. Get Sexy! Not for your: husband, boyfriend, kids, or anyone else! Do it for you! Be your own motivation because you are enough of a reason!
2. Break out of "the box" of "I can't" that you've created due to physical characteristics that you can't change anyway.
3. Be content! Stop comparing your life to others: Just live YOUR life! Your only competition should be the you of yesterday.
4. Don't be fooled by what you see on social media. Everyone is not living a more fulfilling, more enjoyable life than you...And even if they are, remind yourself of Point #3.
5. Accept compliments by simply replying with a smile and saying "Thank you!" That's it! No more, no less!
6. Know your worth! You have value and it is independent of anything that you own and anything that you've ever accomplished. You are more than the sum total of your material possessions and life's accolades. Your value is in being simply and uniquely you.

Encouragement: I've called this a journey because it is. There is no final destination and I will never "arrive," but instead, I'm forever aiming to do better than I did the day before. So, don't be discouraged and quit because you don't get "it" right away! Old habits "die hard!" Keep at it and celebrate each day's "wins!"

The Journey to Self Love

Campaign: "Sex Me Over"

No, you're not reading the same chapter as the previous one. This campaign addresses something entirely different. In this chapter, I step into the bedroom. I guess you could say this chapter is one for the wives and those desiring to be wives one day...

As I previously mentioned, low self-esteem can negatively impact a variety of areas in your life. In addition to what I've already discussed, another area I struggled with was inside my bedroom. I realize that "bedroom talk" is usually considered a taboo topic, but part of the reason I struggled for as long as I did was because very few Christians talk about this! I don't know if it's out of fear or embarrassment, but the lack of honest, open communication regarding this subject is what keeps wives bound and marriages suffering. But don't put the "white cape" on me yet because full disclosure: I was hesitant to include a chapter about sex in my book. I was afraid and embarrassed (Go figure!). I was afraid of what people might say and/or think and I was embarrassed that I might be the only person struggling. But, I know better! I know that my journey might be unique, but oftentimes our struggles are universal. If I've struggled with confidence in my bedroom, I'm sure there are other women struggling as well. So I decided to include this chapter because I want to be a help to others and also because it was part of my journey to self-love. Remember: Self-Love also involves your self-esteem and low (or high) self-esteem affects every area of your life, INCLUDING your sex life and I would be remiss to not include a discussion on it. So, in the name of transparency and honesty, let's talk sex!

I can write a whole book on the "Sex Me Over" Campaign (maybe in the future)... Building self-confidence in the bedroom was the hardest thing to implement and overcome of all the previous campaigns. In fact, I'm still challenged in this area today. I've had to do a lot of un-learning and re-learning. Allow me to explain...

As I shared earlier, I grew up a church kid, a "PK" (Preacher's kid), a "good girl." Christianity wasn't just something my parents forced upon me. Again, even at a young age, I took my salvation very seriously. I was fully vested. (Just so I'm clear: I'm not saying this was a bad thing. At all. Nor do I believe my parents taught me with malice or ill-intention, but that doesn't mean that some unintended consequences wouldn't result--and they did. I appreciate my upbringing and how I was raised. My moral fiber was constructed as a child and it's something that guides me as an adult. These are all good things!). However, I was essentially taught that sex was bad, dirty--nasty even. No, these words were never uttered as overtly as I just expressed, but the underlying tone was there. I didn't realize it at the time, but my mind was consumed with a negative connotation of sex. Couple this negativity with a low self-image and you have a "recipe for disaster" as a married woman.

As a teenager, I was taught the value of my virginity and the importance of not exposing myself to different spirits by having intercourse with several different men. Women are receivers, so by laying down with men who aren't your husband, you are literally opening yourself up to receive different spirits. Have you ever heard of "soul ties?" A "soul tie" is like a linkage (in the spiritual realm) between two people. It links their souls together, which can yield positive or negative results. I was deathly afraid to be linked to someone other than my spouse. So, I held onto my virginity as a teenager and all while I dated my soon-to-be husband.

...But let me not "paint myself" as completely innocent. Kevin and I dated through our teenage years and through college. When I tell you temptation was all around me! My goodness! Did I mention that Kevin was not a virgin? It was a constant battle to try to do the right thing. I often felt like I had to be the stronger person in the relationship to prevent us from "falling into" sexual temptation. It was hard and put a lot of strain on our relationship and on me personally. I never imagined that trying to remain sexually pure until marriage would require so much effort and energy.

Fast forward to June 26, 2004: My wedding day. I was so happy to walk down the aisle and wed the love of my life. Isn't that what every woman (who desires marriage) wants? To marry her best friend?...But how many of us know that after the wedding comes the marriage. A lot of times, we fall in love with the idea of being a bride and we forget that a bride becomes a wife and a wife has responsibilities to her husband. From a biblical perspective, marriage is the only relationship in which sex is permissible. Now consider all of the years of teaching in which I was subconsciously accepting negative falsehoods about sex being: bad, nasty, and not of God! Here I am a married woman and I need to "undo" those years of teachings. NEWSFLASH: It doesn't happen overnight. At all. Couple that with a negative self-image and low self-esteem and there you have the key contributing factors that lead to an unhappy sex life.

As I was going through this season of learning to love myself, I had to confront some of my past beliefs and the teachings that seamlessly penetrated my thought process. I didn't realize how these factors were impacting me until I got married. The teachings lay dormant until it was time for me to be a wife and express myself sexually. I was stuck in my old way of thinking that sex was bad and I needed to hold on to my purity. I somehow believed that virginity--my sexual purity--was next to Godliness, and now in the context of marriage (the relationship dynamic that sex was created for): Here I was struggling! You see: A couple's sex life is a "barometer" (of physical intimacy) for their relationship. Sex, by nature, allows you to be vulnerable. You are literally exposing yourself to your spouse. Marriage is the only relationship where this type of intimacy is ordained.

Back then, in my mind, as long as every other area of my marriage was doing fine, then sex was really unnecessary. I honestly couldn't ask for a better spouse. We had healthy communication, we got along, and we enjoyed each other's company, so my marriage was in a healthy place. Except it wasn't.

When we first got married, I didn't realize how my self-esteem had an impact on our relationship (sex life included), but it did! We never had a big "fallout," but there was definitely always a "lingering residue." There is a certain level of confidence required to have a steamy "marriage bed is undefiled" (Hebrews 13:4, King James Version) type of sex life, and I just didn't carry that level of confidence. There were so many things I didn't like about myself that I couldn't understand how my husband could desire me sexually. I couldn't "wrap my mind" around the fact that he loved me for me. Kevin often tried to reassure me that I was beautiful to him and I was everything he ever wanted in a woman, but at that point in my life: I simply did not believe it. I never felt confident.

I had to learn that sex was not a secondary, inferior need that God designed only for men to desire. (I'm speaking generally here because there are relationships where the woman craves sex more than the man; however, in my situation, the need was greater in my husband than in me). I couldn't figure out how my husband could place so much value on the intimacy of sex; I felt like his need to express his love for me was tied up in a physical expression that I just didn't have. It took me years to understand that the way God created man is different than the way He created woman. Men are not inferior--they're just different. The physical intimacy of the relationship comprises a good fraction of their "love language," while women are typically concerned with the emotional well-being of the relationship. The perfect contrast of each gender's relationship focal points actually "strikes" an ideal balance in creating a healthy relationship, but as women, if we're not careful, we can find ourselves underestimating the importance of (even neglecting) physically intimate encounters with our husbands. We can compartmentalize the various facets of our relationship into categories, leaving sex to be a chore. Sex is not a prehistoric, barbaric desire that only immature men crave. Listen ladies: I believed so many of the wrong things and my marriage was silently suffering daily.

The "Sex Me Over" Campaign (as you can tell) required the most time, energy, discipline, and studying to get things right. It required more of a commitment because I was making a change not only for me, but for my marriage and husband as well...So one of the first things I had to do was learn. Similar to redefining my definition of beauty, I had to redefine my definition of sex based on a Biblical perspective. I began reading books on marriage, sex, God's view of marriage, and how God created man to desire sex. This season was profoundly enlightening and at times--discouraging. Any book related to sex, I would read. The problem was that I would read the books and by the time I finished, I felt discouraged and sometimes defeated. You see, a lot of the books I read (in one way or another) suggested that I was to have sex with my husband so he wouldn't cheat on me and the Bible said so, but let's talk about the problems with this approach.

Problem #1: So he won't cheat...
Can you imagine laying down at night completely exhausted from the day, beside your husband who requires no "start-up?" Men can be exhausted too, but they're always "ready." So your husband gently nudges you (and you KNOW that nudge), but you're tired so you want to decline, yet in the back of your mind are thoughts that if you don't, he'll possibly cheat on you? So you turn over and give a half-hearted attempt at intimacy and while your husband is sexually satisfied, he isn't truly satisfied. With this type of mentality, your thoughts towards sex are negative, which will easily manifest in your bedroom. What you don't want to do is "roll over to be nice." Your husband wants more than your compliance: He wants an active participant. The half-hearted approach will only take you so far until your husband's dissatisfaction becomes a major issue in your marriage. Your resolve to "be nice" may last for a while, but eventually, you will become resentful, just as I did.

Problem #2: Because the Bible says so.
Initially, this may seem like the perfect reason, but let me explain to you why it isn't. Jesus says, "If you love Me, keep my commands" (John 14:15, New International Version). What this scripture really means is that by establishing a relationship with God and really getting to know Him intimately, you wouldn't want to hurt or grieve Him. (If you're married:) Think about the relationship you have with your spouse: You love him, right? You wouldn't want to hurt him intentionally and this feeling is not stemmed from

obligation or "thou shalt nots." There's a genuine place in your heart that says, "I love my husband and I don't want to see him hurt." This is essentially what John 14:15 is saying: Once you know God and have an understanding of His character, knowing what hurts Him, you avoid those things out of your love for Jesus Christ, not simply because "the Bible says so." The very same logic is true when it comes to intimacy with your husband. I've tried "the Bible says so" route, and honestly, I ended up in the same place as the "so my husband doesn't cheat on me" route--Resentful. By operating in an uneducated mentality, your motivation is not derived out of love, but legalistic obligation. Anything you do out of legalistic obligation is a chore and you'll do it begrudgingly...And again: Your husband wants more than your compliance: He wants you to want him. He wants to feel desired.

My hope in my honesty and transparency is that I'm helping you and encouraging you in-the-fact that you're not alone! For years, I struggled with these issues and it seemed that the books I read led me down the same cycle of guilt, followed by a short-lived action plan, followed by resentment, and then I eventually gave-up...Not to mention I was too embarrassed to ask for help. Everyone seemed to have their marriage all together, yet here I was: Struggling. Lo and behold, there are plenty of women who struggle with this very issue, but never utter the words aloud. My hope is that as I move into the next section, you're equipped with information and empowered to make changes that last a lifetime.

The Healthy Way to Think About Sex:
There are so many things I wish I'd known during the early years of my marriage (and if we're being honest: There are a lot of things I wish I could unlearn from my childhood). Sex is so much more to men than the physical act: It is

also about love. Sex is one of the primary ways a man communicates love to his wife. When we, as women, constantly decline our husband's advances, we are actually communicating a lack of love. "Eye-opener" right? I read a book early on in my marriage journey called *The 5 Love Languages*[1]. The author, Gary Chapman, discusses the five primary ways to show and receive love, which include: Acts of Service, Words of Affirmation, Physical Touch, Gifts, and Quality Time. Now think about this: What if your husband denied you the ability to receive love in the way in which you communicate? What if your love language is quality time (which is one of mine) and your husband decided that spending time with you is not a requirement to show love? What if he constantly avoided spending time with you? How would that make you feel? How long would your relationship last? Would you feel loved? When we deny our husbands sex, they ask themselves the same questions and feel that same lack of love. I know it's "a hard pill to swallow." You might even be coming up with a ton of excuses as to why your love language is more superior than physical intimacy and why your relationship can be sustained without sex, but listen to me: Sex is THAT important to men. This truth took me a long time to understand and equally as long to embrace. But once I did, I honestly felt convicted because I love my husband and I wasn't showing him love in the way he understood and could receive. The revelation I gained from my conviction wasn't prompted by obligation, but was the direct result of not wanting to hurt someone who I love. I was motivated to change, but even this wasn't enough. I had to "ignite the sexual spark in me" in order to keep the initial momentum going. There were 3 things I had to come to realize:

1) I am a sexual being and I should listen to my body.
I had to accept that I AM, in fact, a sexual being! That's right! The "good girl," who in some ways had sworn off sex

and thought of sexual intimacy as the untamed part of man, finally had a mindset shift regarding the fact. The fact of the matter is that God created me as a sexual being just as much as he created my husband. Ultimately, I had to "stir up" my inner sexual urges in order to satisfy his needs and establish a healthy relationship and a long-lasting marriage.

As women, we play many different roles in life: mother, wife, sister, best friend, employee, entrepreneur, etc. By the end of the day, we're tired and drained, mostly craving lots of sleep. I get it. Most days I could fall asleep at 8:00pm, but on rare occasions, there are those times when you feel your sexual juices "flowing," but how many times do you ignore those desires? How many times do we blatantly ignore those feelings because we're tired? Well, allow me to challenge you to fully indulge those feelings? It will not only please your husband, but by listening to your body, you are training yourself to embrace and cultivate your sexual prowess more and more, which then increases your level of comfortability with this innate desire.

2) I really had to learn how to initiate sex. Yes, ladies: Initiate, which may be challenging and even feel awkward at first, but this will help to ignite your sexual prowess as well. Initiating sex puts you in control, a feeling that is not only empowering, but also sexy! You'll feel it. Put aside all of your inhibitions and just let go! This is probably one of the hardest things to do consistently, especially if you grew up a "good girl," but I promise you your husband will forever reward you for exercising reciprocity in the area of sexual initiation. Initiation is one of the most powerful ways to impact your sex life. Men want to feel "wanted" and "desired," so the act of initiation is the single most impactful way to demonstrate to your husband that you're not only interested in sex, but that you're sexual attracted to him.

3) Finally, I had to learn to change the way I responded to my husband's advances. Yes, another mindset shift is required. You must teach yourself that sex is not a chore. Chores are household tasks that are assigned to you: Things that must be done, but not necessarily things you want to do. Sex becomes a daunting task when viewed from the "wrong lens" and God didn't intend for it to be that way. Sexual intimacy with your husband should be enjoyable and something you look forward to in your relationship. In fact, in order to maintain a healthy marriage, it's a necessary component. Going back to *The Power of Charm*'s "act as if" principal, sometimes you will have commit your body and allow your feelings to follow. To be clear, I am NOT saying, "lay down and be nice" (laying down and being nice is providing a warm body for your husband, but you're not an active, interested participant). Changing the way you respond is not something that will happen overnight because some days, you just won't feel like it; however, I encourage you to commit your body (be present and an active participant) and eventually, your feelings will catch up.

A lot right? Believe me, I know, but I don't want to leave you feeling burdened with guilt, so let me give you some practical advice: Educate yourself first! Knowledge truly is power, so learn! Pick up a few Christian books that discuss God's view on marriage and sexual intimacy. If you don't know where to start, I suggest: *The Good Girl's Guide to Great Sex*[2] by Sheila Wray Gregoire and *For Women Only*[3] by Shaunti Feldhahn. I've read plenty books on the subjects of men and sex, and honestly, these two are the only ones that didn't leave me feeling discouraged.

Secondly, "get out of your own head!" Going through the "campaigns" in the order that I've laid out is vital because once you deal with your own physical insecurities, you (current wives & future wives) can truly move into sexual freedom and confidence. Don't worry about your body not being perfect because NO ONE'S body is perfect, so don't get "hung up on" minor details. Just set out to enjoy yourself and be vulnerable with the one person who you can be completely open with. Marriage is such a beautiful thing, it really is! Enjoy it and everything it has to offer!

Ultimately: "JUST DO IT!" I promise, Nike couldn't have penned a more perfect tag line! It really is that simple: JUST. DO. IT. You don't need to lose any weight, you don't have find the perfect outfit, or wait for this or that… You can find a million and one excuses and not one will be good enough. The sexual health of your marriage is important and you shouldn't neglect or ignore it. The health of your marriage is dependent on it and your husband will appreciate it too! Decide to make a small, yet sustainable change.

Point-of-Reflection: Sex is one of the most taboo topics in the Christian community. You're mostly told, "don't do it until you're married," but what's often forgotten about is what to do when you do eventually get married. Take this opportunity to evaluate your disposition toward sex and educate yourself on how to do better. Ask yourself if you're demonstrating love to your husband in the way in which he understands, and if you're not, ask yourself: "What are some ways that I can do better?"

Encouragement: Don't beat yourself up! This is an area of opportunity (for constructive growth) in your marriage. Instead, make up your mind to educate yourself and then develop an action plan to do better.

Epilogue

Can I put it plainly for you? I was terrified to write this book! My own insecurities and "hang-ups" had me "enclosed in a box" for far too long and fear had an intense grip on my life. I had dreams of speaking to women and encouraging them to reach their highest level of potential, but all I ever did was dream. I would pray and pray, asking God to allow my dreams to become my reality, yet year after year, nothing happened. Why? Why wasn't this happening for me? The answer is quite simple: God isn't a magician. He doesn't just wave a wand and say magic words, and things just happen...(Now don't mistake what I'm saying: God is sovereign and He can certainly can do whatever He wants, whenever He wants, but He doesn't operate like a genie in a bottle). I had to put in some work and "elbow grease" into my own dream (Hebrews 11:1, New International Version, is a great reference point for-the fact)...And this book is my "elbow grease."

I share my story with you because I want you to know you're not alone traveling on this journey of self-love. While my story is unique, my struggle with low self-esteem and feelings of low-self worth are quite common. I can relate to you if you've ever felt: discouraged, defeated, unloved, and ugly. I vividly remember days I cried out to the Lord, wondering why He made me the way that He did.

Thankfully, the more I continue to "walk with God," the more I'm reminded of His intentionality--in life's good and not-so-great seasons--in each of our lives. Gospel artist, Travis Greene, serves us up with a great reminder of God's constant goodness with his single: "Intentional." Nothing God does is by mistake. His love is relentless for us all and God has been so gracious in allowing this book to even be, evidence that there has been great purpose in my tears.

I implore you: Allow yourself the opportunity to become your best self by embarking on this journey of self-love. I make no promises that it'll be easy, in fact I encourage you to prepare for its challenges, because the road isn't always easy. You'll have good and bad days (feeling like you've "nailed it" at times and other times: Maybe not so much), but know that it's ok! There are peaks and valleys in every journey. Don't let the obstacles stop you from trying. The manifestation of undeniable joy in your life makes the journey more than worth it.

I hope you don't, but you may feel slightly overwhelmed, because you're excited and you want to embark on this journey, but I highly recommend you pace yourself from day-to-day! Know this: The journey is a marathon--NOT a sprint--and there is no final destination. Don't try to accomplish everything in one week or even one month. I started out over seven years ago and I still have my hills and valleys, and some days, I have to go back to the basics and tell myself "I'm worth it." One key factor that I want you to remember is that consistency is what will yield the results you desire to see as you work on cultivating both your inner and outer confidence. Consistency leads to permanent and healthy changes in your life.

Ultimately: The most important thing is that you get started! Begin your personal journey of confidence--inside and out--and make steady progress in every moment of the journey!

Notes & Recommended Reading

The Message and The Messenger
1. *Miss Representation.* Dir. Jennifer Siebel Newsom and Kimberlee Acquaro. Perf. Christina Aguilera, Michele Bachmann, and Chris Baker. Girls' Club Entertainment, 2011. Film.

A New & Improved Me!
1. *What Not to Wear.* TLC. 18 Jan. 2003 - 18 Oct. 2013. Television.
2. John P. Hewitt. *Oxford Handbook of Positive Psychology.* Oxford University Press, 2009 (pp. 217-224). Print.

Campaign: "You Are Worth It!"
1. Ron Arden and Brian Tracy. *The Power of Charm: How to Win Anyone Over in Any Situation.* AMACOM Books (1st edition), 2006. Print and via Kindle.

The "Love On" Challenge
1. *Keeping Up with the Kardashians.* E! 14 Oct. 2007 - Present. Television.

Campaign: "Get Sexy!"
1. Eva Mendes. Interview. *EXTRA.* NBC: 18 Mar. 2015. Television.

Lessons Learned...
1. "Intrinsic." *Merriam-Webster.com.* 2011. http://www.merriam-webster.com/dictionary/intrinsic
(3 Jul. 2016).

Campaign: "Sex Me Over"

1. Gary Chapman. *The Five Love Languages.* Northfield Publishing, 1995. Print.
2. Sheila Wray Gregoire. *The Good Girl's Guide to Great Sex.* Zondervan, 2012. Print.
3. Shaunti Feldhahn. *For Women Only.* Multnomah, 2004. Print.

Epilogue
1. Travis Greene. "Intentional." *The Hill.* Pendulum, 2015. CD, Digital Download.

Made in the USA
Monee, IL
10 January 2021